This I Believe

A Legacy of Biblical Truth

Thomas William Bray

sermontobook.com

Copyright © 2016 by **Thomas William Bray**

All rights reserved. No part of this publication may be reproduced, distributed, or transmitted in any form or by any means, without prior written permission.

Scripture quotations marked (ESV) are taken from The ESV® Bible (The Holy Bible, English Standard Version®) copyright © 2001 by Crossway, a publishing ministry of Good News Publishers. ESV® Text Edition: 2011. The ESV® text has been reproduced in cooperation with and by permission of Good News Publishers. Unauthorized reproduction of this publication is prohibited. Used by permission. All rights reserved.

Scripture quotations marked (KJV) are taken from the King James Bible. Accessed on Bible Gateway. www.BibleGateway.com.

Sermon To Book
www.sermontobook.com

This I Believe / Thomas William Bray
ISBN-13: 978-1-945793-07-3
ISBN-10: 1-945793-07-4

For God's Glory and Our Good.

CONTENTS

Called to Preach 3
I Believe in God 9
I Believe in Jesus 23
I Believe Sin Is Real 39
I Believe in Salvation Through Christ 51
I Believe the Bible 61
I Believe in Missions 73
I Believe in Heaven 85
Notes 95
About the Author 98
About Sermon To Book 100

INTRODUCTION

Called to Preach

A cool spring breeze tussled the shock of black hair and ruffled the collared shirt of the 23-year-old Arkansas man as he stood on the riverbank, shuffling the cigarettes in his hands. Decidedly, he tossed the package into the current and watched them float away. He would never pick up another cigarette for the rest of his life.

The previous Sunday afternoon Thomas Bray had told his wife, Clorean, they should attend a church service that evening. Although they were not regular church attendees, she agreed to go. That evening, Bill Lewis, a local Baptist pastor, preached with fiery passion, and the conviction of the Holy Spirit fell upon Thomas. The following week, Bill Lewis and a church deacon came to visit the Brays. Thomas was still under the conviction of the Spirit. By God's grace, Thomas was saved that day.

As he stood on the riverbank watching his cigarettes float away, he felt a hunger in his heart to live for the glory of the God, who had saved him from the death his sins deserved. That passion, to live and be used for God's glory, became the foundation of his call to preach just a few months later.

Thomas was ordained and called to his first pastorate at Liberty Baptist Church in Walker, Arkansas, on July 26, 1951. He was empowered by the Spirit of God in his preaching. Though only possessing a fifth-grade education, he had the intellect and mental prowess of a brilliant orator. His sermon notes were scribbled on scraps of paper just large enough to fit unobtrusively in his Bible and yet, as He preached, his sermon resonated with the power of the whole Bible—drawing references, illustrations, and detailed explanations with seamless ease. He was a gifted man who humbly acknowledged, "The Lord has been good to me. I don't understand why I was able to do what I did. The Lord was just so good to me."

Thomas loved preaching and accepted every invitation to preach. In forty years of pastoring, from 1951 to 1991, he preached in nearly two hundred revivals across Missouri, Arkansas, Kentucky, Illinois, and Wyoming. He traveled to Jamaica twice to preach on mission trips. After retiring from the full-time pastorate, he continued to preach in churches, serving as an interim until the churches could find a permanent replacement. For five consecutive summers, he traveled to Wyoming to do interim work after his retirement. Thomas continued preaching until his health would not allow it.

When asked if he ever thought about leaving the ministry, he replied, "I never even thought to quit!" Preaching was his life's work. Preaching was his calling—his passion. There is nothing Thomas would rather do than preach the Word of God to the people of God.

Devoting himself to the study of Scripture, he poured over the text all week in order to preach two to three times a week. He avidly consumed books that he believed would aid his understanding and preaching. He also took advantage of a Bible degree program at Williams Baptist College to grow in his understanding of theology as well as his skill in preaching. His preaching was developed from regular reading of the Scripture, which affected him deeply. Working through the text, he would divide it up and prepare the message, always keeping it a secret lest the Devil find out.

His greatest joy as a pastor was the fellowship he experienced with the Lord in the study and in the pulpit. He loved the Lord and loved His Word.

When asked what advice he would give young pastors, he stated unequivocally, "Pray. You must be a man of prayer, seeking the Lord for freedom to preach but also to challenge and encourage you." Thomas devoted himself to prayer, like so many faithful men of the past, and experienced great power in the pulpit. His favorite theologian was the English Prince of Preachers, Charles Haddon Spurgeon. Thomas always said that Spurgeon could do more with the Scripture than any man he ever read.

The hardest part of ministry for Thomas was the constant strain of the weekly deadline. Rarely, if ever, did he take a Sunday off. One of his struggles today is longing to preach without being able to. He aches to preach as a man with a fire in his bones and yet is physically unable.

Nonetheless, Thomas has left a legacy of preaching. His three sons all became pastors, as well as two of his grandsons. His second son, Tom, once asked him, "Dad, would you pray for me to have the liberty, energy, and freedom in preaching like you have?" Thomas was an exemplary preacher whose fiery eloquence God used in the conversion of many sinners and the edification of countless saints. He was a man of great pulpit skill and great intellect. God used this man to make a lasting impact upon countless lives, most especially his family. Many of his children and grandchildren are faithfully serving the Lord to this day.

In this short volume, you will be introduced to the preaching and theology of Thomas William Bray. This book is adapted from a series of messages he preached, entitled *What I Believe*. Not only will you be introduced to his pulpit skill and intellectual prowess, but you will also hear his heart. He explains the doctrines that have shaped his life and ministry with biblical fidelity, startling clarity, and powerful conviction.

Following each main chapter of this book, we've added a workbook section with reflective questions and application steps. These sections are included for your use in independent reflection, discussion with a friend, or group study, as you further your commitment to practicing the eternal truths that Thomas Bray preached. Thomas Bray has had and will always have a lasting impact upon our lives. We love him more than words can express and respect him as a father in the faith as well as our own grandfather. We believe you will be blessed, encouraged, and instructed by this book.

For God's Glory and Our Good,

Phil Bray and Luke Bray

November 2016

Thomas William Bray

CHAPTER ONE

I Believe in God

Several years ago, I met a man who said, "Preacher, I would like to ask you to do something for me. Could you just explain God for me?" Now, that's not your usual storefront conversation, but I did my best to answer him. It's not every day God presents you with such a divine appointment, and when He does, you just have to do your best and let God do the rest.

I told the man, "If I could explain God to you this morning, He would be an awfully little God because that would reduce Him to something finite we could fully comprehend. But friend, God is neither little nor finite. God is the Almighty. He is the disposer of the events of all history, the controller of all time and eternity. God has everything in His control. I am incapable of fully explaining God to you, but I declare to you that I believe in God. God has revealed Himself to me by His Holy Spirit and by His Word through His Son, the Lord Jesus Christ.

I have no better proof to offer you than what God has done in my own life. God has touched my life, and that touch has changed my life. I am not the same person that I was before I met God, and because of that, I know beyond any question that there is a God. To fully explain God is to attempt the impossible, but to declare Him is explicit joy. There is no greater joy in life than to declare that I believe in God, God loves me, and I am His. God's purpose for you and for me is that we might seek Him with our whole hearts, that we might desire Him, and that we might search out after Him until we find Him.

The Names of God

God is our goal and our reward. We are to seek Him until we find Him, and as we seek, we continue to learn more and more of who God is. Our God is many things. In this chapter, we'll examine a few of those things. We'll scratch the surface of who exactly our immeasurable, matchless God is.

God Is Jehovah, "I AM"

In Exodus 3, we have the story of Moses' commissioning. God seeks Moses out to tell him to lead the Israelites out of Egypt, and during their conversation, Moses asked God in whose name he will be sent. God tells Moses, "I AM WHO I AM" (Exodus 3:14 ESV). The Hebrew word for "I AM" is "Jehovah." Our God declares Himself to be Jehovah. As the Old Testament unfolds, the Bible expands on God's name. In four separate stories, we see God's name described in four distinct ways.

God Is Jehovah Jireh, "The Lord Will Provide"

In Genesis 22, we read the story of Abraham's faithfulness. In verse two, God commands Abraham to sacrifice his only son, his promised child. Abraham sets out to do as God has commanded, telling Isaac that "God will provide for himself the lamb for a burnt offering" (Genesis 22:8 ESV). Abraham moves to complete the sacrifice as required, but the Lord stays his hand. Abraham looks up to see that "behind him was a ram, caught in a thicket by his horns. And Abraham went and took the ram and offered it up as a burnt offering instead of his son. So Abraham called the name of that place, 'The LORD will provide'" (Genesis 22:13–14 ESV), Jehovah Jireh. On that day, God provided for Abraham, and He continues to do the same for us today.

God Is Jehovah Nissi, "The Lord Is My Banner"

In Exodus 17, God has delivered the Israelites from the clutches of Egypt by His mighty hand, and the Israelites have embarked on their forty years of wandering in the desert. As the Israelites wander, God commands them to expel their enemies from the land. In Exodus 17, the Israelites have clashed with the Amalekites. As the Israelite men went out to meet the Amalekites, Moses stood "on top of the hill with the staff of God" in his hands (Exodus 17:9 ESV). As the men fought, Moses' arms grew tired of holding up the staff. As long as the staff of God was lifted, the Israelites prevailed. So as Moses' arms grew tired, Aaron and Hur "held up his hands, one on one side, and the other on the other side" (Exodus 17:12 ESV). To worship the Lord and to remind them all that the Lord had won the battle, "Moses built an altar and called the name of it, The LORD Is My Banner" (Exodus 17:15 ESV), Jehovah Nissi. That day, the Israelites fought under the banner of the Lord; He was their authority and source of power, and He is the same for us today.

God Is Jehovah Shalom, "The Lord Is My Peace"

In Judges 6:11–27, God calls Gideon to lead the Israelites against the Midianites. As Gideon speaks with an angel of the Lord, he questions God's authority and provision. In resistance to the Lord's call, Gideon asks for a sign that the Lord is indeed speaking to him. He offers the Lord a gift of goat meat, goat broth, and unleavened bread. The angel accepts the gift on behalf of the Lord, and Gideon sees the situation more clearly. He built an altar there to honor the Lord, calling it "The Lord Is Peace," Jehovah Shalom. The Lord offered Gideon peace to carry out his calling of defeating the Midianites, and God offers each of us the same today: the peace to complete the tasks to which He calls us.

God is Jehovah Shammah, "The Lord Is Present"

In Exodus 33:14–15, the Lord promises Moses that His presence will go with Moses. God fulfills this promise by visibly leading the Israelites through the desert, taking the form of a pillar of cloud by day and a pillar of fire by night. God rested His visible presence over His tabernacle and went before them as they made their way. For the Israelites, and for us today, the Lord is present, Jehovah Shammah. How wonderful, how comforting, to know that even today, God is with us.

As the Israelites wandered through the desert, they experienced their God in each of these ways, just as we can today. As the Israelites prepared to end their wandering, their leader, Joshua, reminded them, "Hear, O Israel: The Lord our God, the Lord is one. You shall love the Lord your God with all your heart and with all your soul and with all your might" (Deuteronomy 6:4–5 ESV). There are not many gods; there is only one God, and He is Jehovah. He is our Lord, and He is with us.

Explaining God

Our one true God, Jehovah, is unified in His personality, will, and purpose but has revealed Himself in three distinct ways: Jehovah is Father, Son, and Spirit.

God Is a Holy Trinity

Though God is one, He fulfills these three distinct roles, each an integral part of His identity as Jehovah.

We, each created in His image (Genesis 1:26), are plural in our nature as well. Our plurality is more concrete than God's, so consider our nature as an example of that of our God. When we read in the Bible, we find that we are plural in our nature. We have a body; we have a soul. We have flesh, and we have bones. These parts of ourselves are distinctly separate though they create one whole. In 1 Thessalonians, Paul prays that "your whole spirit and soul and body be kept blameless at the coming of our Lord Jesus Christ" (1 Thessalonians 5:23 ESV). We are pluralistic in our nature. I am one integrated unit of distinct parts, just as God is Himself.

In Genesis 1:26, God refers to Himself in the first-person plural: "Let *us* make man in *our* image, after *our* likeness" (Genesis 1:26 ESV, emphasis added). In doing so, God is acknowledging the three distinct mediums of His self-revelation.

In turn, we can't truly know God in one of His three natures without knowing the others. For instance, no one comes to the Father except through the Son (John 14:6)—Jesus, the living Word, who "was with God" and "was God" from the beginning (John 1:1 ESV). Jesus was the Word made flesh (John 1:14), or God "in human form" (Philippians 2:8 ESV). And after Jesus was resurrected, God the Father sent the Holy Spirit to us in the name of Jesus (John 14:26). The Spirit makes the Son, and by extension the Father, precious and real to us. Thus, each of God's three forms is inextricable from the others, and each makes possible our relationship with the others.

God Is Eternal

Our God, Jehovah, exists outside the confines of time and space. Our God is eternal. In Psalm 90:2 (ESV), Moses prays, "Before the mountains were brought forth, or ever you had formed the earth and the world, from everlasting to everlasting you are God." From everlasting to everlasting He is God. In Deuteronomy 33:27, Moses refers to God as "eternal," and in Malachi 3:6, God Himself declares that He "[does] not change." Genesis 1:1 tells us that in the beginning, God. From everlasting to everlasting, there has been God because He is the eternal one. He exists outside of the bounds of time, and He never changes. He has been and will ever be our God, Jehovah: Jehovah Jireh-Provider; Jehovah Nissi, our banner and authority; Jehovah Shalom, our peace; and Jehovah Shammah, present with us.

God Is Love

In 1 John 4:7–8 (ESV), the apostle John exhorts us to "love one another, for love is from God, and whoever loves has been born of God and knows God. Anyone who does not love does not know God, because *God is love*" (emphasis added). In the words of John, the beloved disciple, God is love. It's a simple sentence: God is love. Its structure tells us that its two parts are synonymous: God and love are the same thing. And as John tells us, the two are inseparable. We cannot know God without love, and we cannot love without God because God *is* love.

One of the oldest questions of all time is "Does God really love me?" The Bible answers this question with a resounding and simple yes. In John 3:16 (ESV), the beloved disciple writes: "For God so loved the world, that he gave his only Son, that whoever believes in him should not perish but have eternal life." In Romans, Paul tells us that "God showed his love for us in that while we were still sinners, Christ died for us" (Romans 5:8 ESV). Paul goes on to say, "He who did not spare his own Son but gave him up for us all, how will he not also with him graciously give us all things?" (Romans 8:32 ESV).

God so loved the world that He spared not His Son but delivered Him up for us all, that He might freely give us all things. God so loved us that He sacrificed His own Son, the Lord Jesus Christ, and offered Him up on the cross of Calvary for your sins and for my sins, that we might have forgiveness. Why? Friend, there is no explanation except the fact that God loves us.

The Creator of the universe—the One who spoke this world into existence, the One who placed man upon the earth personally—loves you, even while you are yet a sinner. I know myself better than I know you, and when I look at myself, "Wretched man that I am!" (Romans 7:24 ESV), I cannot help but wonder how God could love me that much. But He does. And now I call Him Savior. I'm His son, and I belong to Him. He's my God, my heavenly Father.

Prayer

Father, how inadequate we are. Words are so shallow. Often, God, we find that when we want to exalt You, we don't have what we need to be able to express what's on our hearts and minds. And so now, Father, I pray that despite this, if there is someone reading these words who needs to know the one true God, help them to know You as the one true God and Jesus Christ as Your Son. Father, become real to someone today. Adopt someone into Your family today; become their Father just as You are mine. In Jesus' name I pray. Amen.

WORKBOOK

Chapter 1 Questions

Question: How do you usually characterize or think about God? How does your habitual understanding of God line up with the truth about Him?

_____
_____
_____
_____
_____
_____
_____
_____
_____
_____

Question: When have you experienced God's presence in your life most clearly? How did you know He was there?

_____
_____
_____
_____
_____
_____
_____
_____
_____
_____

Question: How can you deepen your relationship with the Holy Spirit?

_____
_____
_____
_____
_____
_____
_____
_____
_____
_____

Action: Believe! Hold fast to your faith in God as your creator, provider, powerful lord, and source of peace. Amid the trials and triumphs of life, remind yourself that God is eternal. Find your proof of His existence and goodness in what His presence accomplishes in your own life. Seek to know God, and avoid the temptation to reduce Him to fit a mold the unbelieving world can readily accept. Trust in His love, and know Him better by practicing love as you pursue a relationship with Him in all of His forms—Father, Son, and Holy Spirit—without disregarding any of the Holy Trinity.

Chapter 1 Notes

CHAPTER TWO

I Believe in Jesus

There has been no greater influence on history than the person of Jesus Christ. His existence is so pivotal that the very way we measure time hinges on His birth. Regardless of your belief or disbelief in the person of Jesus and what He stands for, He is a central figure in history. No other figure is so polarizing, and if we claim to be Christians, our entire identity hinges on what we believe about who He is. I want to point you to the Lord Jesus and see you come to know Him, love Him, follow Him, obey Him, live for Him, and let Him be Lord of your life.

Jesus Is God's Son

If we want to see God, we're going to have to see His Son, the Lord Jesus Christ. Jesus Christ, Jesus of Nazareth, Jesus the Lamb of God, was the spitting image of His Father because "He is the image of the invisible God, the firstborn of all creation" (Colossians 1:15

ESV). We look upon the face of Jesus Christ and behold the glory of God in the person of Jesus Christ. He is the very Son of God.

Jesus Is Fully Man and Fully God

It's not enough for us to just say, "Yes, Jesus truly is a man sent from God." Jesus was a man, but He is so much more; He is God come down to us in human form. In John 3, we learn of someone who struggled with this issue. Nicodemus, a Pharisee, comes to see Jesus at night. Nicodemus was a very well-educated man. He recognizes that Jesus acts on God's behalf, but he struggles to understand that Jesus is God. Nicodemus says, "Rabbi, we know you are a teacher come from God, for no one else can do these signs that you do unless God is with him" (John 3:2 ESV). Many people today respond to Jesus in the same way. They believe He's just a teacher, even if sent by God, but they deny that He *is* God.

Friends, that is not enough. Jesus gets frustrated with Nicodemus. He says "Are you the teacher of Israel and yet you do not understand these things? Truly, truly, I say to you, we speak of what we know, and bear witness to what we have seen, but you do not receive our testimony. If I have told you earthly things and you do not believe, how can you believe if I tell you heavenly things? No one has ascended into heaven except he who descended from heaven, the Son of Man" (John 3:10–13 ESV). Nicodemus couldn't understand things he'd seen with his own eyes. Jesus' response is to chastise

Nicodemus for his unbelief because it was Nicodemus's responsibility as a teacher of religion to understand and interpret heavenly things. As a heavenly being Himself, Jesus is the only person qualified to teach heavenly things. His conversation with Nicodemus asserts His authority to speak: Jesus is both a heavenly witness and an earthly witness, uniquely qualifying Him to teach truth.

In Philippians, Paul writes:

> ...though [Jesus] was in the form of God, [He] did not count equality with God a thing to be grasped, but emptied himself, by taking the form of a servant, being born in the likeness of men. And being found in human form, he humbled himself by becoming obedient to the point of death, even death on a cross. Therefore God has highly exalted him and bestowed on him the name that is above every name, so that at the name of Jesus every knee should bow, in heaven and on earth and under the earth, and every tongue confess that Jesus Christ is Lord, to the glory of God the Father. — *Philippians 2:6–11 (ESV)*

Jesus emptied Himself. That means that Jesus, though He was God, gave up being God to become a man and dwell among us—all on our behalf.

Jesus Is Without Sin

The role of an Old Testament High Priest was to intercede with God on behalf of the people, "For every high priest chosen from among men is appointed to act on behalf of men in relation to God, to offer gifts and sacrifices for sins" (Hebrews 5:1 ESV) The priest stood between God's anger at sin and sinful people, offering sacrifices as just settlements for the debt owed God from sin.

Human priests are appointed by God to deal with the wayward and lead them to righteousness. Jesus became man so that He'd be eligible for God's appointment as high priest. God appointed Him to the office. "And being made perfect, [Jesus] became a source of eternal salvation to all who obey him, being designated by God a high priest after the order of Melchizedek" (Hebrews 5:9–10 ESV).

Paul explains it best:

> This makes Jesus the guarantor of a better covenant. The former priests were many in number because they were prevented by death from continuing in office, but he holds his priesthood permanently, because he continues forever. Consequently, he is able to save to the uttermost those who draw near to God through him, since he always lives to make intercession for them. For it was indeed fitting that we should have such a high priest, holy, innocent, unstained, separated from sinners, and exalted above the heavens. He has no need, like those high priests, to offer sacrifices daily, first for his own sins and then for those of the people, since he did this once for all when he offered up himself. — *Hebrews 7:22–27 (ESV)*

Jesus, God Himself, is eternal and perfect, both in His human and heavenly forms, which makes Him uniquely qualified to hold the office of High Priest indefinitely. He acts eternally as our perfect intercessor before the throne of heaven.

Jesus Is Our Savior

Jesus can serve as our forever intercessor because He offered the perfect offering for sin: Himself, the blameless firstborn. His sacrifice saved us, and "there is salvation in no one else, for there is no other name under heaven given among men by which we must be saved" (Acts 4:12 ESV). Jesus did not sin. He chose to give up His blood—to give up His life. He shed His blood for your sins and for mine, not for His own because He had none. In so doing, He became the perfect covering for our sins. Our sins are hidden underneath the blood of the Lord Jesus. Our sins are obliterated. They are taken away; they will never be remembered against us again because God has cast them "as far as the east is from the west" (Psalm 103:12 ESV). God will never look upon the sin of a believer again by the blood of Jesus Christ.

Jesus Is Lord

If we can affirm the Lordship of Jesus in our lives, oh what a difference it would make in this community and around the world as we allow Jesus Christ to be Lord. Because God has already exalted Him and lifted Him up and given Him a name; He has seated Jesus at His own right hand. And Jesus Christ is therefore reigning in heaven in full authority, having power over this universe. But there is still the little realm of your heart that Jesus needs to control—to which only you can give Him access.

Jesus Is an Exalted Ruler

God has given Jesus a name that is above every other name: "…at the name of Jesus, every knee should bow, in heaven and on earth and under the earth, and every tongue confess that Jesus Christ is Lord, to the glory of God the Father" (Philippians 2:10–11 ESV).

Jesus Is a Sovereign Judge

Jesus is going to come one day as the sovereign judge of all men. "When the Son of Man comes in his glory, and all the angels with him, then he will sit on his glorious throne. Before him will be gathered all the nations, and he will separate people one from another as a shepherd separates the sheep from the goats" (Matthew 25:31–32 ESV). The sheep and goats represent the righteous and the unrighteous, and on that day, each and every one of us will have to give an account of our actions. We will be weighed. We will be sifted. We will be judged. That day is coming "because he has fixed a day on which he will judge the world in righteousness by a man whom he has appointed; and of this he has given assurance to all by raising him from the dead" (Acts 17:31 ESV). The day is coming when Jesus will reveal Himself in all His glory, as both man and God, High Priest, Savior, and Lord.

Jesus was a man. History says He lived thirty-three years in Palestine before dying on a Roman cross. He claimed to be God Himself, sent to earth to save us all. Do you believe Him? Everything depends on that one decision. Do you believe Jesus is who He says and has done and will do as He says? There are only two things you can do in response to Jesus: you either receive Him as Lord and Savior, or you reject Him, turn Him away, and refuse Him as Lord of your life. If we could recognize and know who Jesus is, we would fall on our faces like Isaiah of old, prostrating ourselves, and we would cry out, lament, confess, acknowledge our sinfulness, and allow Him to purge our lives and cleanse us from our iniquities if we just continue to be willing.

The Miracle of the Virgin Birth

The Bible also teaches that Jesus was born of a virgin (Luke 1:26–37). Understanding how this works is not essential to your salvation, but believing that it did happen is. It is one thing to not understand the virgin birth, but it is another thing to deny and refute the virgin birth—because when you say you do not believe in the virgin birth of the Lord Jesus, you are repudiating the Word of God. The Holy Scriptures are complete, perfect, and inerrant, so you are denying the truth if you take the position of not believing in the virgin birth of the Lord Jesus. The Bible asserts that Jesus Christ was born of a virgin; therefore, accepting the Bible as truth requires accepting the reality of Jesus' virgin birth.

The Virgin Birth Is Mysterious

The concept of a virgin birth is a mystery that largely defies understanding. We do not accept or reject things on the basis of not understanding them because our finite brains cannot grasp the infinite mind of God. There are many things in the Word of God I don't completely understand, but I do believe them because they are in the Word of God. If I read it in the Bible, I know it is true.

Jesus' conception is not the first time God fulfilled a promise of a seemingly impossible conception. Jesus was born of a virgin, and Isaac of the Old Testament was born of parents who were too old. As part of God's covenant with Abraham, He promised Abraham's descendants would outnumber the stars in the sky. But Abraham and Sarah had long since passed their childbearing years without a child. God visits again to remind Abraham of His promise, and "Sarah laughed to herself, saying, 'After I am worn out, and my lord is old, shall I have [the] pleasure [of bearing a child]?'" (Genesis 18:12 ESV). She couldn't see how she could possibly conceive, but God's response was, "Is anything too hard for the LORD?" (Genesis 18:14 ESV). There isn't anything too hard for the Lord. There is not anything the Lord cannot do, including conceiving a child within a virgin. The virgin birth is a mystery we can accept only because we believe in God, the Bible, and what the Bible teaches. We must accept Jesus' birth on faith.

The Virgin Birth Was Miraculous

The Israelites face a foreign army in Isaiah 7. The Lord sends Isaiah to prophesy victory over their enemies. The Lord encouraged Ahaz to ask a sign of God's power, and Ahaz wisely declined to test the Lord. In response to Ahaz's faithfulness, through Isaiah, the Lord promised Ahaz a sign: "Behold, the virgin shall conceive and bear a son, and shall call his name Immanuel" (Isaiah 7:14 ESV). The Lord fulfilled His promise in the miraculous birth of the Lord Jesus Christ, conceived in Mary by the power of the Holy Spirit, born to become the Savior of the world.

This is one miracle God will not repeat. It had never been done before, and it will never be done again. God chose to confine Himself to the form of a baby and come to earth to save us all. This act is two miracles in one: Jesus' actual miraculous conception, and His miraculous choice to be conceived at all. The miracle is this: the great, eternal God, creator of the universe, elected—by His own sovereignty—to humble Himself and become a man. But He didn't just appear as a man. No, He chose to be born into this world, using a woman as He'd created her to bring Him into this world as a baby.

We choose to reject God's revelation of Himself to the world if we reject the virgin birth. We choose to reject the miraculous if we reject the idea that God could be born a baby, grow to be a man, and dwell among us. It is more than miraculous that God would be willing to become a man, to be born of the Virgin Mary, to live a perfect, sinless life, and to become the Savior of the world. The virgin birth is a mysterious miracle, but it's so much more, too.

The Virgin Birth Is a Message

The prophet Isaiah had much to relate about the Messiah, the immediate future of the Israelites, and the end times. God kept him busy. In chapter 7, we read that the messiah will be born of a virgin (Isaiah 7:14). In chapter 9, we learn:

> *For to us a child is born, to us a son is given; and the government shall be upon his shoulder, and his name shall be called Wonderful Counselor, Mighty God, Everlasting Father, Prince of Peace. Of the increase of his government and of peace there will be no end, on the throne of David and over his kingdom, to establish it and to uphold it with justice and with righteousness from this time forth and forevermore. The zeal of the LORD of hosts will do this. —*
> **Isaiah 9:6–7 (ESV)**

Matthew 1 tells us how God finally accomplished all He'd promised. An angel appeared to Joseph, Mary's betrothed, and explained, "'She will bear a son, and you shall call his name Jesus, for he will save his people from their sins.' All this took place to fulfill what the Lord had spoken by the prophet: 'Behold, the virgin shall conceive and bear a son, and they shall call his name Immanuel' (which means, God with us)" (Matthew 1:21–23 ESV).

The message of the virgin birth is just this: God is with us. God is with us. If this same God could miraculously place a baby in the womb of a virgin, the same God can work miracles in you, too. Nothing is too hard for the Lord. There are many ways God could have come into this world if He'd so chosen. He could've come in any way at any time to do away with all the evil of humanity, but instead He chose to take on human form, come as a baby, born of the virgin Mary in Bethlehem. He came as Jesus, Emmanuel, God with us, so that we might know Him, learn of Him, and come to live for Him.

Prayer

Father, thank You for the opportunity I have to examine Your Word. Please help me to respond to Your Word, and by the power of the Holy Spirit, to place my strongest confidence in the truth of Your Word. I'm thankful that I believe Jesus Christ is truly Your Son, our Lord, who alone lived without sin. I know, Father, that anyone who will not come to You through Your Son cannot come at all. Thank You for the miracle of His virgin birth through Mary, and thank You that He grew into the man who sacrificed Himself on the cross for the sins of the world. Thank You for giving me life in Your Son because I know that He is the source of life. Open my eyes fully to the light of the gospel, to the light of Your truth, so that I might clearly see Jesus, our Savior. In Jesus' name I pray. Amen.

WORKBOOK

Chapter 2 Questions

Question: What aspect of Jesus or salvation is most difficult for you to understand fully? What is the best way to respond to this uncertainty or incomplete understanding?

Question: In what ways was (and is) Jesus fully God? In what ways was He fully human? Why is it important that He lived as a man?

_____
_____
_____
_____
_____
_____
_____
_____
_____

Question: What exactly is your relationship with Jesus? What is the next step you need to take with Him?

_____
_____
_____
_____
_____
_____
_____
_____
_____

Action: Find your salvation in Jesus, even if your mind doesn't fully grasp the intricacies of His nature or the workings of His saving power. Simply accept that He was fully man, yet fully God, and died in your place. Praise Him for being perfect and without sin, yet sacrificing Himself to save us. Likewise, accept the miracle of His virgin birth and let Him work miracles in your life as well. In all things and at all times, find God and find life through your loving relationship with Jesus Christ.

Chapter 2 Notes

CHAPTER THREE

I Believe Sin Is Real

The Bible is full of wonderful ideas, touching stories, and hope. But the Bible also has many things to say to us about sin. It'd be easy for us to only talk about the pleasant things, but then we'd miss a major purpose of the Bible: warning us about sin. Today, many of us, even believers, do not take the severity of sin seriously. We are not thoroughly convinced that a day will come when we will suffer the consequences of our sin, whether in this realm or the eternal.

Proverbs 14:9 (ESV) tells us, "Fools mock at the guilt offering, but the upright enjoy acceptance." We, like the fools of the proverb, look so tritely upon sin. We tell stories and make jokes about sin, and the Bible says that when we do that, we are a generation of fools! God will not look with favor upon the life of any individual who lives in sin. You cannot live in sin and enjoy God's favor because sin is a serious affront to God. Romans 6:23 (ESV) tells us that "the wages of sin is death," a spiritual death of eternal separation from God. When you allow sin to come into your life and take hold, when you do not repent and turn to God, you will be cut off from the favor of God.

There is absolutely no way that we can ever justify even one sin. God will not overlook any sin. He will forgive by the blood of Jesus, but He will not overlook even one unconfessed, unrepentant sin. The experiences recounted in the Bible are relevant even today, and our Bible tells us about three kinds of sin.

Presumptuous Sins

The frustrations in the lives of the people in the Bible are much like yours and mine. They are much like those the apostle Paul experienced. In Psalm 19:12–13 (ESV), David asks, "Who can discern his errors? Declare me innocent from hidden faults. Keep back your servant also from presumptuous sins; let them not have dominion over me! Then I shall be blameless, and innocent of great transgression." Keep your servant from presumptuous sins. These presumptuous sins are the ones that just engulf a person. They destroy the whole person, enslaving him in all the ways of wickedness in this world. Presumptuous sins are bold and arrogant, rash and willful.

All of us commit presumptuous sins, and it's important for us to remember that the same God who poured out His judgment on the presumptuous sinners of times past looks down on us and our presumptuous sins today. In Isaiah, God calls His prophet to pronounce His judgment on such presumptuous sinners. Isaiah warned:

> *Woe to those who draw iniquity with cords of falsehood, who draw sin as with cart ropes, who say: "Let him be quick, let him speed his work that we may see it; let the counsel of the Holy One of Israel draw near, and let it come, that we may know it!" Woe to those who call evil good and good evil, who put darkness for light and light for darkness, who put bitter for sweet and sweet for bitter! Woe to those who are wise in their own eyes, and shrewd in their own sight!* — **Isaiah 5:18–21 (ESV)**

Sinners caught in presumptuous sins spurn the council of God.

These presumptuous sins lead people to ignore God and disregard His Word, statues, and commandments. As long as people remain caught in sins of presumption, they will disregard God and dig themselves deeper into their own sin. Peter explains that "the Lord knows how to rescue the godly from trials, and to keep the unrighteous under punishment until the day of judgment, and especially those who indulge in the lust of defiling passion and despise authority. Bold and willful, they do not tremble as they blaspheme the glorious ones" (2 Peter 2:9–10 ESV). God can deliver us from sins of presumption, but as long as we remain in such sin, we even speak evil of God without fear.

In Proverbs 14:34 (ESV) we learn, "Righteousness exalts a nation, but sin is a reproach to any people." The openness of sin in our day should make us tremble. There is no way the lewd, shameless, presumptuous sins of our time will escape God's judgment. We must be aware of the sin around us, and like David, we must beseech God to reveal and forgive our hidden faults, to keep us from presumptuous sins, to not let those sins and faults have dominion over us.

Secret Sin

Openness regarding our sin requires a level of vulnerability that we as humans struggle with. We prefer to keep our sins private, hidden, but there is no way to hide something from God. In Psalms 90:8 (ESV), Moses prays, "You have set our iniquities before you, our secret sins in the light of your presence." Moses is acknowledging that God sees everything. If we think that we can be secretive about our sins, hide them, cover them up so that God cannot see, then we are very foolish. The Bible makes it plain that there is no way you can hide from God—not even if you're Moses hiding out in Midian or Jonah fleeing on a ship.

God will not allow one of His children to sin without coming to search out the one who is lost, without coming to correct that child's ways. God will not leave you in your sin because sin leads to more sin. Sin separates us from God, and He will not allow us to go long without confronting us by the power of His Holy Spirit. Just as God sought out Adam and Eve in the garden after their fall, God, in His infinite love and compassion, will seek us out to correct us in our sin.

God is not a delinquent Father. He loves His children too much to leave them to their own ways. His purpose for every believer is to conform to the likeness of His

Son. God's purpose for your life is to make you like Christ, and that cannot happen while you wallow in sin. God will deal with you and your sin. He will correct you to restore you to the ways of righteousness and obedience. Even David, man after God's own heart, committed grave, secret sins. He committed adultery with Bathsheba, then arranged her husband's death so he could marry Bathsheba and legitimize the pregnancy resulting from their affair (2 Samuel 11:1–5). David suffered the consequences of his decisions, but God loved him too much to allow him to continue down the path he was on. God corrected David and led him back to the ways of righteousness, even as David lived with the aftermath of his choices. Just like David, we will experience the consequences of our sins, but God loves us too much not to correct us and lead us back to righteousness.

Greater Sin

In the New Testament, Jesus speaks of a "greater sin." In John 19:11 (ESV), Jesus references this greater sin directly at His sentencing hearing with Pontius Pilate, saying "You would have no authority over me at all unless it had been given you from above. Therefore he who delivered me over to you has the greater sin." Jesus doesn't fault Pilate for doing his job; instead, He says those who rejected Him, delivering Him into Pilate's hands, have committed a greater sin: rejecting the truth of Jesus Christ as Messiah.

Sins can be forgiven. If you confess your sin and ask for forgiveness, God will grant your request. God is faithful to forgive you and cleanse you from all unrighteousness. But those sins are only forgiven if you've not committed a greater, unforgiveable sin: rejecting the Lord Jesus Christ as your Savior.

You cannot know God and reject His Son. You cannot be born of God and not receive His Son as your Savior. All the sins we've discussed are forgivable. Every single one, even murder, can be forgiven. There will be consequences for our sins, but they can be forgiven.

Yet there is no forgiveness for the individual who realizes that Jesus Christ is the Son of God; that He came into this world to die on a cross for his or her sins, taking that individual's sins upon Himself; that He was buried for three days but rose on the third day a living Savior; and that He lives and reigns on. The one who recognizes all of this and hears Jesus calling, but still rejects the gift Jesus offers, is the one who commits the greatest sin—rejecting Jesus as God's Son and our Savior. The good news is that, despite our presumptuous and secret sins, Jesus is calling.

Prayer

Lord, I am imperfect—a sinner. Despite my failures, Lord, I pray that You will use my words to draw people closer to You. Quicken my heart, Lord. Convict me of my attitude toward sin. Convict me of my compromises, Lord, and my pleasure in my sins. Lord, thank You for loving me despite my many faults and failures. Your Word tells us that if we but admit we are sinners, believe in Jesus, and repent our wicked ways, we will be saved. Thank You, Lord, for saving us. In Jesus' name I pray. Amen.

WORKBOOK

Chapter 3 Questions

Question: When have you thought or acted as if you knew better than God? What was the result?

_____
_____
_____
_____
_____
_____
_____
_____
_____
_____

Question: How open are you about your sins and sinfulness? To whom do you need to confess or admit your sins?

Question: How exactly can you ensure you don't commit the great sin of rejecting Jesus Christ or the Holy Spirit?

Action: Recognize the reality of sin, and be open in confessing your sins and sinfulness. Don't presume to know better than God and His Word! Above all, seek forgiveness of your sin through Jesus and His sacrifice on the cross, avoiding the greater sin of rejecting Him.

Chapter 3 Notes

CHAPTER FOUR

I Believe in Salvation Through Christ

The concept of salvation is absolutely essential to understanding the Christian faith. Our entire belief system hinges on accepting salvation as it is explained in the gospel. In his letter to the Romans, Paul explains that he is "not ashamed of the gospel, for it is the power of God for salvation to everyone who believes, to the Jew first and also to the Greek" (Romans 1:16 ESV). Salvation is for everyone, and it is personal.

After Jesus was born, there was an audience of angels and shepherds to commemorate the birth of a savior. And then they all went home, and Jesus' life on earth as the child of first-century Jewish parents began. According to custom, Jesus' parents took Him to the temple to be purified, and while there, the first experience of Salvation with Jesus is recorded. Simeon was a faithful Jew to whom God had promised that "he would not see death before he had seen the Lord's

Christ" (Luke 2:26 ESV). The Holy Spirit sent Simeon to the temple as Jesus' parents were arriving, and God's promise to Simeon was fulfilled. Simeon held Jesus "in his arms and blessed God and said, 'Lord, now you are letting your servant depart in peace, according to your word; for my eyes have seen your salvation that you have prepared in the presence of all peoples, a light for revelation to the Gentiles, and for glory to your people Israel'" (Luke 2:28–32 ESV). For my eyes have seen your salvation. Simeon knew that God would show him salvation before he died, and true to His word, God allowed Simeon to recognize in the infant Jesus his savior. Just as Simeon discovered, salvation must become a personal experience before it can be understood.

Salvation Is a Person

Simeon recognized the person of his salvation. For years, he had been waiting for the consolation of Israel. For years, he had been a faithful servant of the Lord in the temple, a devout man faithful to God, but even years of service had not given him the experience of a personal salvation through the Lord Jesus Christ. But when he held the infant Jesus, he blessed God and said, "my eyes have seen your salvation" (Luke 2:30 ESV). Simeon waited for years to receive the promised peace of the Lord, and he recognized the Savior he'd been waiting for in Jesus the Messiah. He realized the promised peace only after encountering the person of salvation. As long as people are looking outside the person of Jesus Christ for their salvation, they cannot find it. Salvation is in the Lord, and only in the Lord.

Many professed Christians have not yet come to know salvation in the person of Jesus Christ because they still struggle with the plan of salvation. A "plan" of salvation is a misnomer. The Bible tells us clearly that salvation is not in a plan but rather is in the person of the Lord Jesus Christ—and that is why so many people struggle with Christianity. They find it void and empty, purposeless and powerless. A salvation "plan" has no power to change or influence their lives because without Jesus, that "plan" of salvation will never come to fruition.

A plan of salvation is a series of steps or ideas created by man, and those plans change. But if you come to the person of salvation, if you receive the Lord Jesus Christ as the Master in your life, you will find fulfillment, purpose, direction, and power because as you receive the Lord Jesus, you are empowered by God not only to become but also to be a person of God.

It's not a matter of whether you're baptized, or join a church. It's not a matter of trying to do the best you can or observing the ordinances of the church. It's not a matter of being the very best person you know how to be, because none of those things have ever saved anyone. But the person who, like Simeon, encounters Jesus and recognizes the source of salvation will be saved.

Salvation Is of the Lord

Without coming to know salvation in the person of Jesus Christ, we cannot be forgiven of our sins or reconciled to God, now or in eternity. As Jesus Himself said:

> *I am the way, and the truth, and the life. No one comes to the Father except through me.* — ***John 14:6 (ESV)***

In the Old Testament, we read the story of Jonah, a prophet who resisted the call of God in his life. In disobedience, Jonah ran from God, and his ensuing punishment placed Jonah in the belly of a fish for three days. In the pit of his despair, in the literal "belly of the beast," Jonah cries out "Salvation belongs to the Lord!" (Jonah 2:9 ESV). Only after Jonah's declaration of repentance is he delivered from the belly of the fish to complete the task God had prepared for him.

Jonah's experience is a picture of how the Lord works out our own salvation. The Lord works out our salvation. It's His to give—and He offers it to us through His Son.

Salvation Is Permanent

Our salvation is of the Lord and in the Lord, and when we come to know the salvation that is in Jesus Christ, we have come to the assurance of the permanence of our salvation. Hebrews 5:9 (ESV) tells us that "being made perfect, [Jesus] became the source of eternal salvation to all who obey him." In the Lord Jesus Christ, there is eternal life. There is eternal salvation, and when you come to know that salvation, it's not just for a moment, a day, a year, or even a lifetime. Salvation is eternal and will usher you into the Lord's presence forever.

Salvation Is Powerful

In the person of Jesus Christ is the power of salvation, the power to change your life, and the power of God to make you a new creation that comes only as you receive the gospel of the Son of God (2 Corinthians 5:17). Only as you come to know the gospel of Christ who came to live and to die, to be buried and to be raised again as your living Savior, can you know the power of salvation. Jesus has the power to make you a new creature, to make you a new person, to give you a new nature, to give you a new spirit, and all of this is realized as you come to know salvation in Jesus Christ through the truth of His gospel.

The Bible declares the necessity of salvation by God comes as a result of your sin. The Bible says that "the wages of sin is death, but the free gift of God is eternal life in Christ Jesus our Lord" (Romans 6:23 ESV). The only way to experience freedom from sin is to encounter Jesus and trust in His salvation—this coming to know and trust Jesus is what salvation is all about.

Do you know Him? Have you come to know Him through the truth presented in the gospel? Have you come to know Him personally, as Simeon did? Can you, like Simeon, say "my eyes have seen your salvation" (Luke 2:30 ESV)? Salvation is not by proxy. It's not by family. It's not by church. Salvation is an individual experience as, one by one, God's spirit speaks to our hearts and enables us to see Jesus as our Savior if we are willing to call on Him.

Prayer

Father in heaven, I pray that You would help me, as Your child, not only to know that I have been saved, but also to live like I have been saved. I pray that I would learn to enjoy the salvation of the Lord—that I would know His deliverance and power in my life. Lord, I am grateful that I can know the source of this power through the gospel. There is no other name, no other way, no other person of salvation except the Lord Jesus Christ. In Jesus' name I pray. Amen.

WORKBOOK

Chapter 4 Questions

Question: Where do people often look for salvation? Where besides Jesus have you looked in the past? How did you recognize your error?

_____
_____
_____
_____
_____
_____
_____
_____
_____
_____
_____

Question: What does it mean that salvation through Christ is "permanent"?

Question: To what extent do you live as if you're saved? In what areas of your life do you fall short of living as a person saved by God's grace? What, then, is your next step for growth in living out your salvation?

Action: Salvation is personal! Accept the necessity of seeking salvation from God, and don't look for salvation anywhere but in the person of Jesus. Then trust in the power and permanence of your salvation in Christ—while also living each day and each moment as someone who has, indeed, been saved!

Chapter 4 Notes

CHAPTER FIVE

I Believe the Bible

In 2014, several information-gathering organizations completed studies of how Americans view and use the Bible. A Gallup poll revealed that 75 percent of Americans believe the Bible is directly connected to God, but only 28 percent believe the Bible should be taken literally.[1] A Barna study from 2014 revealed that despite the stated beliefs of three-quarters of our population regarding the Bible's divine association, only 26 percent read Scripture with any regularity.[2] The Barna study concluded that this disparity is a result of skepticism—that despite being generally acknowledged as connected to God, many are skeptical of the Bible's trustworthiness. If released data for 2016 are any indication, this trend is not improving.[3]

What good does it do to believe the Bible is the Word of God and yet never read it, never look into it to find out what God has to say to us? Dwight L. Moody, a nineteenth-century evangelist, said, "The Bible will keep you from sin, or sin will keep you from the Bible."[4] We'll address our beliefs of sin in a later chapter, but this quote from Psalm 119:11 (ESV) resonates: "I have stored up your word in my heart, that I might not sin against you." The Bible has a specific role: It is an antidote to sin, but it is so much more than that.

The Bible Is God's Word

The role of the Bible in the lives of its readers is significant: The Bible is the very Word of God. It is the written account of who our Creator is, what He values, and what He will accomplish on Earth and in our lives. God inspired the Bible. He gave these words to chosen, holy men who, in turn, gave them to us in written form, and "All scripture"—every single word—"is breathed out by God…" (2 Timothy 3:16 ESV). As discussed in the previous chapter, our God is eternal, and He doesn't change. The Bible, the Word of God, is consistent with its author; God's Word is eternal and does not change, or as Psalm 119:89 (ESV) describes, "Forever, O LORD, your word is firmly fixed in the heavens." The Bible is God's eternal, living Word, and we can trust in it.

The Bible Is True

The 2014 Barna study indicates that the generations rising into adulthood disengage from Scripture because of doubt. In a world dominated by relative truth, the concept of a single Truth that exists outside our beliefs and opinions is difficult to grasp, so their response is to doubt its authenticity. The authenticity of the Bible is directly related to the authenticity of its author. Just as we can trust in who God is, we can trust that what He says in His Word is true. Our God is faithful, and the measure of His faithfulness is His Word. What God has said in His Word is true. What God has promised in His Word will be fulfilled. God is faithful to His Word. Though the Bible was written by fallible men, these men were acting in faithfulness to an infallible God. God, by His Holy Spirit, spoke to these men. In faithfulness, these men transcribed the words God gave them. These men were not authors of scripture in the modern sense; rather, they acted as scribes to create a tangible copy of God's words as spoken to them. The result of God's inspiring these men is an entire book, thousands of pages, of God's Words, preserved for us in written form without error. Despite the nature of the hands who wrote them, these words are a perfect, infallible message to us from a flawless God.

In Isaiah, we read:

> *For my thoughts are not your thoughts, neither are your ways my ways, declares the* LORD. *For as the heavens are higher than the earth, so are my ways higher than your ways and my thoughts than your thoughts. For as the rain and the snow come down from heaven and do not return there but water the earth, making it bring forth and sprout, giving seed to the sower and bread to the eater,* **so shall my word be that goes out from my mouth; it shall not return to me empty, but it shall accomplish that which I purpose, and shall succeed in the thing for which I sent it.**
> *— Isaiah 55:8–11 (ESV, emphasis added)*

God said as surely as the rain comes down from heaven to water the earth and make things grow, so shall His Word be. No one argues where the rain comes from or that it comes to make things grow. No one argues that that same water will return to the clouds in a different manner than it came. Just as certain as the rain, just as certain as the water cycle, God's Word is true. It *will* be fulfilled. God says that His Word will accomplish that which He purposed. It shall do as He intends and will not return void. The mission God lays out in His Word cannot fail, and His mission is clear: that all may know Him.

The Bible Is Personal

In the Old Testament, God lays out His plan for the world. First Kings 8:60 (ESV) explains that God's intention is "that all the peoples of the Earth may know that the LORD is God; there is no other." Ten times we read variations of the phrase "that all may know" (Joshua 4:24; 1 Samuel 17:46; 1 Kings 8:43; 1 Kings 8:60; 2 Kings 19:19; 2 Chronicles 6:33; Job 37:7; Psalm 67:2; Psalm 83:18; Isaiah 37:20). God's plan is that each and every one of us, all of us, come to know the truth of God as defined by the Bible. The Bible, while intended for a universal audience, is intensely personal.

The Bible Is Practical

Whatever is in the Bible, whatever God's Word tells you to do, you can do; it can be applied. Second Timothy 3:16–17 (ESV) tells us, "All Scripture is breathed out by God and profitable for teaching, for reproof, for correction, and for training in righteousness, that the man of God may be complete, equipped for every good work." God's intention for scripture is to reveal Himself that we may endeavor to become increasingly righteous, to become increasingly like Christ. The Bible's purpose is fundamentally practical.

The Bible Is Life-Changing

The mark of an authentic encounter with the God of the Bible is coming away changed. As we study and pursue the righteousness outlined in Scripture, we will become increasingly conformed to the image of our Creator. James 1:22–25 (ESV) admonishes:

> But be doers of the word, and not hearers only, deceiving yourselves. For if anyone is a hearer of the word and not a doer, he is like a man who looks intently at his natural face in a mirror. For he looks at himself and goes away and at once forgets what he was like. But the one who looks into the perfect law, the law of liberty, and perseveres, being no hearer who forgets but a doer who acts, he will be blessed in his doing.

James said when we look in that mirror, if we are not corrected by it and if we are not somehow prompted by what we see to do something about our condition, it's not going to profit us anything. Now if you sit here reading this and do nothing, if you do not choose to become a doer of the Word, content to be a hearer of the Word only, it's not going to profit you anything. When you accept Christ, you are saved, once and for all. But that moment of salvation is the beginning of a lifelong pursuit of imitating your Master. After choosing to accept God's gift, after choosing to join His family, it's time to get to work. We ought to be doing something. Other translations of 2 Timothy 3:16–17 replace the word "complete" with "perfect" (KJV). This word may be better explained as "mature." The result of applying Scripture to your life is maturity, becoming full-grown in your faith. Many of us are content to just be saved and have little desire to mature, let alone become full-grown. Maturing requires experience, often discomfort, and sometimes even pain.

If your discipleship is not costing you anything, you need to look at your discipleship. Becoming a disciple is choosing to follow someone as your teacher and mentor. The result of following a mentor is to become like the mentor yourself. If your mentor is Jesus, but you do not resemble Him, you need to examine how you're following your mentor. In John 15:18 (ESV), Jesus instructs, "If the world hates you, know that it has hated me before it hated you." If you are living as Christ lived, your actions will make people uncomfortable in their own sin, and they will not like it. They may persecute you to avoid addressing the pull your behavior has on their own consciences. If your discipleship isn't costing you anything, you need to look at your discipleship. Let's take God at His Word. Let's apply His Word to our lives, to our principles. Let's live by His Word. The test of your belief in the Bible is what you do with the truths it contains.

Prayer

Father in heaven, help me to understand Your Word. Allow it to speak to my heart. If I or anyone reading this is living in conflict with Your Word, please speak to us. Instruct us, reprove us, encourage us. We've read in Your Word that all Scripture is profitable for doctrine, for reproof, and for instruction in righteousness. Father, I pray that all of us reading this will pursue Your righteousness and apply the truth of Scripture to our lives. Lord, thank You for the gift of Your Word. Thank You for loving us enough to show us how to live. In Your name I pray. Amen.

WORKBOOK

Chapter 5 Questions

Question: What different perceptions, attitudes, and beliefs about the Bible and its authority have you encountered in your family, workplace, school, neighborhood, or church?

_____
_____
_____
_____
_____
_____
_____
_____
_____
_____

Question: Which elements of Scripture do you find especially challenging to accept fully as God's Word?

How can you come to understand and accept these aspects of His truth?

_____
_____
_____
_____
_____
_____
_____
_____
_____
_____

Question: What part of the Scriptures do you find especially difficult to practice in your daily life? How can you learn the way God wants you to live out or apply this particular part of His Word?

_____
_____
_____
_____
_____
_____
_____
_____
_____

Action: Ensure that your discipleship—your life of following Jesus—is real by ensuring it's costing you something and by following God's Word! Don't let the world tell you the Bible is not real or relevant. Instead, ground your thoughts, words, and actions in its enduring power, authority, and truth. Pray for God's help in applying its wisdom. Remember that the truth is eternally relevant—so if it seems impractical, that's only because you're not practicing it! Let God change your life as you study His Word in Scripture.

Chapter 5 Notes

CHAPTER SIX

I Believe in Missions

As of 2016, the world's population was approaching 7.5 billion people. That same 7.5 billion people includes 11,485 people groups, people who are grouped by similar cultural values and shared language. Of those 11,485 people groups, 6,782 people groups are considered unreached, meaning that less than 2 percent of their populations adhere to evangelical Christian beliefs. Of those 6,782 unreached people groups, 3,021 are considered unengaged, meaning there is no recognized missionary effort in contact with those groups.[5]

Those unengaged and unreached people groups comprise as many as 204 million people who have absolutely no access to the gospel of Jesus Christ.[6] If we include the number of people who live in areas with little Christian identification, there are 3.1 *billion* people in this world with little to no access to the gospel.[7]

Over three billion people! Living in a nation saturated with the gospel gives us an inaccurate perception of how much of the world desperately needs to hear the good news of Jesus Christ. Because there are quite literally churches on every corner in many places in the Western world, we lose sight of the fact that in other places, churches may be hundreds, even thousands of miles apart. We content ourselves to not look beyond the edges of our own little worlds, at the eternal expense of the lost outside them.

Until the 7.5 billion people living on this earth become personalized as individuals to us, they will be nothing more than an abstract figure in our minds. We will not become personally involved in reaching these people as long as we continue to think in terms of billions. If we can catch a vision of each of these people as distinct individuals, seeing them through the eyes of Jesus, filled with compassion and concern, we will commit ourselves to the task of reaching them for the gospel as we believe, go, share, and serve.

Believing

The good news of Jesus Christ is that regardless of who people are or what they've done, God will save them if they believe Jesus is the Son of God and choose to accept Him fully as their Savior. As we mobilize ourselves for the task of reaching the world with this message of salvation, we must first believe in the message ourselves. In Romans 1:16 (ESV), Paul explains that he is "not ashamed of the gospel, for it is the power of God for salvation to everyone who believes, to the Jew first and also to the Greek."

Within the gospel of Jesus Christ, therefore, is enough power to save the world. Every lost person in the world could be saved if given the opportunity to believe, but first we must believe ourselves.

In fact, God commands "that we believe in the name of his Son Jesus Christ and love one another, just as he has commanded us" (1 John 3:23 ESV). How are people going to believe in someone that they've never heard about? How can people receive someone they don't know to believe in? Whether they know it or not, there are people in your community and communities around the world who are waiting to hear the good news of Jesus Christ in a personal, unadulterated way. It is our responsibility to share what we know of Jesus Christ's saving power so that these people may be saved.

Going

God could use any mechanism He chooses to make Himself known so that we may believe. He chooses to send us. We cannot be satisfied to sit comfortably within our church buildings, expecting the lost to come and find us. God's command is to go. He commands us to go anywhere and everywhere to share our message of who God is and how much He loves us. It's not a matter of what people do with the message: God commands us to go and share. What people do with the message we share isn't our responsibility. Going and sharing, however, are our responsibility.

In Isaiah 6:8 (ESV), we read of God commissioning Isaiah to his task: "And I heard the voice of the Lord saying, 'Whom shall I send, and who will go for us?' Then I said, 'Here I am! Send me.'" God had a big job for Isaiah. He sent him to prophesy and rebuke the Israelites, but the first step of Isaiah's job was simply to go. Like Isaiah, each of us must go, whether across the street or around the world. The first step of obedience is simply to go.

Sharing

And he called the twelve together and gave them power and authority over all demons and to cure diseases, and he sent them out to proclaim the kingdom of God and to heal. — *Luke 9:1–2 (ESV)*

After we have believed ourselves and stepped out in faith to go where God sends, our task is to share. In Isaiah 6:9–10 (ESV), God continues to instruct Isaiah in his task:

And he said, "Go, and say this to the people: 'Keep on hearing, but do not understand; keep on seeing, but do not perceive.' Make the heart of this people dull, and their ears heavy, and blind their eyes; lest they see with their eyes, and hear with their ears, and understand with their hearts, and turn and be healed."

Like Isaiah, our responsibility is to speak so that others may *hear*. We are not responsible for anyone's response, but we are responsible for sharing so that people have the opportunity to respond. If we never go, if we never share, then there is no way they can believe as you have believed.

Since the beginning of the church, God's mission for the believer has been to go, sharing His gospel and love along the way (Luke 9:1–2; Luke 10:1–2). In the years immediately following Jesus' resurrection and ascension, Saul was causing serious trouble for the early church, forcing believers to scatter, and the Bible says that "those who were scattered went about preaching the word" (Acts 8:4 ESV). The church includes all believers, not just the preachers. And we should follow the example of the early church, who *all*, as they were scattered by life's circumstances, shared the message of Jesus along the way. The task of sharing the gospel is not set aside for preachers; each of us, working as a part of a larger whole, is to join in the task of sharing the good news of Jesus Christ.

Later on in Acts 8, we read the story of Philip, who headed to the desert of Gaza simply because God told him to. God didn't explain to Philip what he should do or why; He only told Philip to go. And Philip went. As Philip obeyed, God sent an Ethiopian eunuch to pass by. In obedience to the Spirit, Philip hitched a ride with the Ethiopian, and God provided an opportunity for Philip to share the good news with this man. God sent Philip *out of his way* for no reason other than to lead this man to Christ. And Philip obeyed, no questions asked.

We should all consider the example of Philip and allow the Lord to send us wherever He wants us to go in order that people may hear the good news of the Lord Jesus Christ. God can use each of us as He sees fit, and each of us is qualified to share the good news of Jesus Christ.

Serve

The final aspect of missions is a willingness to serve. God calls each of us to serve in unique ways. We are each called to believe, to go, and to share, but we are not all called to do the same things all at the same time. Sometimes you will be the one going, the one speaking. Sometimes you'll only be traveling as far as your backyard, and sometimes you'll be traveling to the other side of the world. But when you are not the one going, you still have a role to play in the sending. Each of us has time to give to the cause of spreading the gospel, whether that time is spent going ourselves or whether that time is spent serving others so that they may go.

Going places costs money. Sometimes you will be paying for your own missionary efforts, and sometimes you'll be paying for the efforts of others. There will always be those willing to go, but those willing to go will always need financial help to get there. In the words of William Carey, famed missionary to India, "I will go down, but remember that you must hold the rope."[8] Those of us contributing financially to the missionary efforts of others find ourselves holding the rope that allows them to climb down and share the good news.

Nothing is worth doing if not bathed in prayer. Paul instructs us to "pray without ceasing" (1 Thessalonians

5:17 ESV), which includes praying for our own efforts to share the good news as well as for the efforts of others.

Prayer

Dear Lord, I thank You for giving me a role in what You're doing—a role in bringing the message of salvation to a lost world. Father, I know You are concerned for the lost. You are interested in the lost. You love the lost. Lord, I pray You will burden our hearts with a need to connect the lost to You, to introduce them to their Savior. Lord, give us the opportunities and the willingness to share Your message of salvation so that people might believe and be saved. In Jesus' name I pray. Amen.

WORKBOOK

Chapter 6 Questions

Question: To whom is God calling you to go and share His Word and the gospel of Jesus Christ?

_____
_____
_____
_____
_____
_____
_____
_____
_____
_____
_____

Question: What are the first steps you need to take to reach the people to whom God is calling you?

_____
_____

Question: What do you remember about the way you first came to embrace God's saving grace through Jesus? What is one lesson you can apply from your own experience as you reach out to the lost?

Action: Love the spiritually lost as God does, and see their plight with urgency. Fulfill the Great Commission of Christ in your community and in the world by believing in the absolute, saving power of Christ's love and sacrifice; by going to the lost and needy where they are; by sharing God's truth unashamedly; and by serving God and others in whatever capacity He calls you.

Chapter 6 Notes

CHAPTER SEVEN

I Believe in Heaven

The question of what happens after this life is one that confronts every person, believer or not. Although some believe that this life is all there is, the precious promises of our Lord say otherwise. Revelation describes this place called heaven in great detail. One of the most beautiful pictures we have is in Revelation 21:3–4 (ESV), which tells us that in heaven, "the dwelling place of God is with man. He will dwell with them, and they will be his people, and God himself will be with them as their God. He will wipe away every tear from their eyes, and death shall be no more, neither shall there be mourning, nor crying, nor pain anymore, for the former things have passed away."

Some people, even among those who believe heaven is real, don't attach much significance to heaven because it's too far removed from daily life. I once heard a man describe how, when he was younger, he didn't think of heaven much. Despite being a believer, this man didn't know anyone who'd passed from this world, so he never spent much time thinking about it. As time went on, people he knew started dying. He lost some of his best friends. And then he started losing extended family members. Then he lost his parents. He even lived long enough to see one of his own children die.

He said that after a lifetime of living and losing, he realized that although heaven had once been insignificant to him, it was gradually becoming even more important to him than the remainder of his life on earth. His interest in heaven was directly proportional to the number of his loved ones living there.

Heaven is more than a congregating place for dead loved ones. Heaven surrounds the very throne of Jesus Christ, and *that's* the glory of heaven. *That's* the prize at the end of this life.

Heaven Is a Prepared Place

It's hard to imagine how wonderful heaven will be, but we know that heaven is real, and we know that Jesus has prepared a place for us in it. In John, Jesus tells us that "if I go and prepare a place for you, I will come again and will take you to myself, that where I am you may be also" (John 14:3 ESV). Heaven is a physical place where we can be with Jesus.

Heaven is where Jesus is, but more than that, it will be paradise, a new Eden. God created Eden as a perfect garden, an ideal place to live, and we lost that ideal through sin. Our transition to heaven after death is a welcome in to a new Eden, a restoration of what was lost: a perfect place to live in perfect relationship with God and each other. In our glorified, immortal bodies, we will enjoy the beautiful paradise Adam and Eve lost, and we will inhabit that paradise forever and ever; in the perfected place our Lord is preparing for us, we will enjoy Him forever.

Heaven Is for a Prepared People

As wonderful as heaven is, it has a specific population. Every person will have the opportunity to gain entrance, but not all will be admitted. Revelation 21:27 (ESV) tells us that "nothing unclean will ever enter it, nor anyone who does what is detestable or false, but only those who are written in the Lamb's book of life." The requirement for entry into heaven is having your name recorded in the Lamb's book of life. Friends, the only way to have your name recorded in that book is to have experienced that special preparation for the cleansing blood of the Lord Jesus Christ.

You must be a regenerate believer in our Lord Jesus Christ and you must accept His sacrificial gift on the cross if you wish to enter heaven. Because, you see, heaven is not only a prepared place: Heaven is for a prepared people. And if you've not been washed in the blood of the Lamb, if you've not been born of the Spirit of God, then that place does not belong to you.

Heaven Is Prepared for Fellowship

In this life, we treasure our relationships, troubled as they may be. In heaven, that beautiful paradise, relationships will likewise be of prime importance. In fact, we will have perfect fellowship: We will have perfect, blessed fellowship with our Father. As His adopted sons and daughters, coheirs with Christ, we will all become the family of God. We'll be like Abraham and Isaac, Jacob and Moses; God the Eternal One is Father to us all, and we are the children of the resurrection. It is a place for fellowship where we'll have spiritual union and relationship with the Father and where we'll have spiritual union and relationship with each other, each of us being equal in the sight of God.

In the perfected place our Lord is preparing for us, we will have fellowship with our Lord, and we'll enjoy Him, worship Him, and serve Him. We will have fellowship with one another, and we'll live peacefully with one another, love one another, and enjoy each other to the very fullest extent. There will be no interruption to our fellowship in heaven. It will not be marred nor broken, because when we are in the presence of our Lord, we are like Him.

Heaven Is Prepared for Service

The heaven our Lord is preparing is also a place of service. Revelation 7:15 (ESV) tells us that we will forever be "before the throne of God, and serve him day and night in his temple." Many times, we think of heaven as a place where we'll all just stand around singing God's praises. We certainly will join the heavenly host as they sing, "Holy, holy, holy..." (Isaiah 6:3 ESV) to the Lord, but we will not be idle. The Bible tells us that in this paradise, we will be busy serving our Lord forever. But this service will not be labor. As we serve the Lord in heaven, we will be totally and perfectly fulfilled, and we will enjoy being with Him and serving Him forever.

This kind of eternal existence is something we all have the opportunity to choose. There is not one single person God excludes from this opportunity. As discussed in chapter 7, people might choose to forego admittance into heaven by choosing to reject Jesus as Savior, but God will deny no one the opportunity to choose. There are absolutely no exclusions. Anyone who is willing to hear His voice, believe in Him, call on Him, and come to Him will be saved. Anyone who puts their faith in Jesus and repents of their sins will be saved. There are no exclusions, and God is longing to save each one of us, even to the uttermost ends of the earth.

In Revelation 21:5–6 (ESV), God was seated on His throne and said:

> *"Behold, I am making all things new." Also he said, "Write this down, for these words are trustworthy and true." And he said to me, "It is done! I am the Alpha and the Omega, the beginning and the end. To the thirsty I will give from the spring of the water of life without payment."*

The key word here is "thirst." Those who thirst, those who long for heaven and our Lord, will be satisfied. If they but choose the Lord and His gift of salvation, their names can be added to the Lamb's book of life, and they can gain admittance to eternal life in the paradise of heaven.

Prayer

Father, thank You for this beautiful promise of heaven. As we anticipate Your coming, help us to conduct our lives in all holiness and godliness. Lord, we know that those who choose not to believe are choosing to forego heaven. Put in their hearts, and put in our hearts, a longing for You. Give us a thirst for the water of life that comes from faith in You. In Your name we pray. Amen.

WORKBOOK

Chapter 7 Questions

Question: What do you picture heaven to be like? How does this compare with what we know of heaven from God's Word?

_____
_____
_____
_____
_____
_____
_____
_____
_____
_____
_____

Question: How does fellowship in heaven differ from fellowship in this life? How is it the same? What are a couple of steps you can take to pursue deeper fellowship with God and others in your life now?

_____
_____
_____
_____
_____
_____
_____
_____
_____
_____
_____

Question: What does the reality of heaven teach you about the way we're supposed to live our current lives on earth?

_____
_____
_____
_____
_____
_____
_____
_____
_____
_____
_____

Action: Take heart in the promise God gives us of a life after this—in a real place of fellowship and service that Jesus has prepared for those who believe and follow Him. Each day, seek life now and for eternity in God and in His Son, Jesus Christ. Let your life now be preparation for an eternity of joy, peace, love, and devotion to the one and only God.

Chapter 7 Notes

REFERENCES

Notes

1. Saad, Lydia. "Three in Four in U.S. Still See the Bible as Word of God." *Gallup*. http://www.gallup.com/poll/170834/three-four-bible-word-god.aspx.
2. "The State of the Bible: 6 Trends for 2014." *Barna*. 8 April 2014. https://www.barna.com/research/the-state-of-the-bible-6-trends-for-2014/.
3. "The Bible in America: 6-Year Trends." *Barna*. 15 June 2016. https://www.barna.com/research/the-bible-in-america-6-year-trends/.
4. Moody, Dwight L. *Goodreads*. http://www.goodreads.com/quotes/668373-the-bible-will-keep-you-from-sin-or-sin-will.
5. "PeopleGroups." www.peoplegroups.org.
6. *Ibid*.
7. "Global Summary." *Joshua Project*. Frontier Ventures. https://joshuaproject.net.
8. Carey, William. As quoted in Piper, John, "Andrew Fuller: I Will Go Down If You Will

Hold the Rope!" *Desiring God.* http://www.desiringgod.org/books/andrew-fuller.

About the Author

Thomas William Bray has left a legacy of preaching. His three sons all became pastors, as well as two of his grandsons. His second son, Tom, once asked him, "Dad, would you pray for me to have the liberty, energy, and freedom in preaching like you have?"
Thomas was an exemplary preacher whose fiery eloquence God used in the conversion of many sinners and the edification of countless saints. He was a man of great pulpit skill and great intellect. God used this man to make a lasting impact upon countless lives, most especially his family. Many of his children and grandchildren are faithfully serving the Lord to this day.

About Sermon To Book

SermonToBook.com began with a simple belief: that sermons should be touching lives, *not* collecting dust. That's why we turn sermons into high-quality books that are accessible to people all over the globe.

Turning your sermon series into a book exposes more people to God's Word, better equips you for counseling, accelerates future sermon prep, adds credibility to your ministry, and even helps make ends meet during tight times.

John 21:25 tells us that the world itself couldn't contain the books that would be written about the work of Jesus Christ. Our mission is to try anyway. Because, in Heaven, there will no longer be a need for sermons or books. Our time is now.

If God so leads you, we'd love to work with you on your sermon or sermon series.

Visit www.sermontobook.com to learn more.

Made in the USA
Lexington, KY
03 July 2017